DON'T SMILE UNTIL DECEMBER

and Other MYTHS About Classroom Teaching

DON'T SMILE UNTIL DECEMBER
and Other MYTHS About Classroom Teaching

Peggy Deal Redman

CORWIN PRESS
A SAGE Publications Company
Thousand Oaks, California

For information:

Corwin Press
A Sage Publications Company
2455 Teller Road
Thousand Oaks, California 91320
www.corwinpress.com

Sage Publications Ltd.
1 Oliver's Yard
55 City Road
London EC1Y 1SP
United Kingdom

Sage Publications India Pvt. Ltd.
B-42, Panchsheel Enclave
Post Box 4109
New Delhi 110 017 India

Printed in the United States of America.

Library of Congress Cataloging-in-Publication Data

Redman, Peggy Deal.
Don't smile until December, and other myths about classroom teaching / Peggy Deal Redman.
    p. cm.
Includes bibliographical references and index.
ISBN 1-4129-2552-5 (cloth) — ISBN 1-4129-2553-3 (pbk.)
    1. Teaching. 2. Teachers. I. Title.
LB1025.3.R427 2006
371.102—dc22   2005022376

This book is printed on acid-free paper.

    06   07   08   09   10   9   8   7   6   5   4   3   2

Acquisitions Editor:	Faye Zucker
Editorial Assistant:	Gem Rabanera
Production Editor:	Jenn Reese
Copy Editor:	J. Lynn McBrien
Typesetter:	C&M Digitals (P) Ltd.
Proofreader:	Kevin Gleason
Indexer:	Kathy Paparchontis
Cover Designer:	Rose Storey

Contents

Foreword

Years ago, teaching was a noble profession. Teachers were respected for who they were and how they made students feel. The rewards were usually not immediate. Some came later in life when students realized what they owed to a teacher who believed in them and nourished a spark that became a beacon to their career and life. Some never came. But, somehow, most teachers sustained faith and hope, believing that they were making a difference. Then somehow education seemed to lose its way. Students became empty vessels to be filled with information dispensed by their teachers. Even worse, many people demanded evidence that the facts were successfully implanted. Teachers were no longer trusted to do their jobs, nor rewarded for the subtle influence they made in students' lives. We have now reached a point so poignantly captured by Yogi Berra years ago: "We're lost, but we're sure making great time."

The moment has now arrived when teachers need to reclaim what has been given or taken away. Our country is now spending billions to improve education. But, for the most part, reform efforts are scaling a ladder affixed to the wrong wall. Well meaning intentions are not reaching the classroom nor touching the core of teaching.

This is where Peggy Redman's book enters the picture. It's the right message, written at the right time, authored by the right person. She's not an aloof, head-in-the-clouds academic; she's a hands-on, reality grounded student of the true art of teaching. Even better, she's a gifted teacher with years of experience. She is now a teacher of teachers and doing the job that should have been done all along. She provides proven pedagogical techniques, coupled with a large dose of the true spirit of teaching. I know this because I have seen her in action. I have also followed her career closely for many years. I am her cousin, proud as punch of what she's doing at the University of La Verne to restore teachers' pride in an essential profession.

Peggy's book exposes several myths that have been perpetuated over the years without a close look at the consequences. Myths are important because they give meaning to life and work. But myths cut two ways and can protect worn-out beliefs as well as give zest, buoyancy, and meaning to things we do everyday. The genius of Peggy's book is its ability to debunk misguided myths while, at the same time, reviving and promulgating traditional images that portray teaching as a sacred profession. The spirit of the book's core message is captured in a short quote from Tracy Kidder's (1989) *Among Schoolchildren:*

> Teachers usually have no way of knowing that they have made a difference in a child's life, even when they have made a dramatic one. But for children who are used to thinking of themselves as stupid or not worth talking to or deserving rape and beatings, a good teacher can provide an astonishing revelation. A good teacher can give a child at least a chance to feel, "She thinks I'm worth something. Maybe I am." Good teachers put snags in the river of children passing by, and over the years, they redirect hundreds of lives. Many people find it easy to imagine unseen webs of malevolent conspiracy in the world, and they are not always wrong. But there is also an innocence that conspires to hold humanity together, and it is made of people who can never fully know the good that they have done. (p. 313)

Peggy Redman's book shines light on a hopeful path to help teachers find their way again and reclaim the moral ground that once set their calling apart from other jobs.

—Terry Deal

Preface

One looks back with appreciation to the brilliant teachers,
but with gratitude to those who touched our human feel-
ings. The curriculum is so much necessary raw material,
but warmth is the vital element for the growing plant and
for the soul of the child.

—Carl Jung

I was born into a family of teachers. My mother taught kindergarten and my father was a junior high math teacher. My extended family, numerous aunts and uncles, my brother and sister-in-law, many cousins, and my son and daughter in-law, are teachers, plus scores of friends; teaching is literally in my blood. I have been a teacher for the past forty-five years in a variety of capacities, second grade, middle elementary gifted students as well as ninth-grade algebra students. My heart has been and always will be in the classroom.

I am now a teacher of teachers. I have taught over 1,500 students who have gone on to become teachers, teachers who are making the same difference in the lives of students that my family and I have always made.

During the past twelve years, it has become clear that there are key qualities necessary to become a good teacher. We all know a teacher needs to effectively transmit subject matter and to know how to develop and deliver a quality lesson plan. In addition, the teacher must be able to identify and teach to appropriate standards. While all of these strategies are important, missing is the core of what it means to be a teacher: the quality of humanness, the ability to touch the lives of students. I have always told aspiring teachers that I can teach them how to develop a good lesson, and I can suggest ideas about better classroom management, but I cannot make them real, authentic people. They, alone, bring that to the classroom, and it is absolutely necessary that, to become an effective teacher, a person needs a soul.

Beyond a doubt, teaching is the best profession in the world. Where else can you find a job where you get paid twice: a paycheck and a chance to make a real difference?

The classroom is a complex place. The teacher is responsible for the nuts and bolts of managing the classroom, developing effective lesson plans, collecting lunch money, addressing the standards, taking roll, working with parents, and collaborating with colleagues. The list is endless. Over the past forty-five years, I have struggled, along with my teacher colleagues, against misleading myths about teaching. In the culture of teaching, there are a number of understood, unwritten rules by which teachers live.

Several years ago, while working with faculty to develop a beginning class for teacher candidates, we came across a wonderful book by Lee Bolman and Terry Deal (1994), *Becoming a Teacher Leader.* In this book the reader is introduced to a series of lenses or frames used by teachers to address the complexities of their world. These frames are commonly used by teachers to size up a situation whether they know it or not. The *human resource* frame emphasizes relationships and the importance of a caring, trusting work environment. Most teachers cite this frame as their favorite. The *political frame* identifies the sources of power, the strength of conflict, a perspective often avoided by teachers. The *structural frame* is exemplified by clear goals and rules, critical strategies for teachers in well-managed classrooms. The fourth lens, the *symbolic frame,* focuses on meaning, belief, and faith; things we know are present in the classrooms of exceptional teachers. As Bolman and Deal (1994) state, "The school becomes a way of life rather than merely a place of work" (p. 6). This book emphasizes the power of the symbolic frame in the true meaning of what teaching is all about. False myths that abound can only be laid to rest by substituting positive ones.

This book identifies eight myths (I know there are more) widely accepted by many in terms of what it means to be a successful teacher. Mythology is powerful, and teaching is rife with myths. These myths are propounded in films and popular books, and lay a foundation for the common sense that is part of our profession. Mythology cuts both ways; there are good myths and bad myths. The bad myths are like barnacles on the shell of education and too often lead us astray. We lose our way and grope for better practices.

In this book, each questionable myth will be reexamined and then dismissed. This opens the door to creation of new myths. A revised view of teaching comes into view, stressing the importance of the human connection as the teacher makes a difference in the lives of young people.

INTENDED AUDIENCE

This book has several intended audiences. Certainly it will find a niche in the training of teachers. The student teaching experience and the introductory course of a teacher preparation program are both key places for its use. As university supervisors work with teacher candidates, many of the questions will arise making a new focal point of conversation for seminars.

A second audience is beginning teachers participating in a 2-year induction program. This book gives insight into many of the first-year dilemmas of a novice teacher. As the beginning teacher works with his or her mentor, the chapters provoke jumping off points highlighting intended areas of growth.

A third audience is undergraduate students completing a subject matter preparation program toward a career in teaching. The positive, uplifting approach of the book gives prospective teachers an idea of the potential and the pitfalls that loom in teaching as a career.

A fourth audience is that of the seasoned teacher in the classroom today. Each of us wants to be seen as caring and gifted with the ability to inspire students in life-changing ways. This book rekindles the idealism we felt when first entering the classroom.

ORGANIZATION OF THE BOOK

This book is designed as a portable mentor for use by prospective and beginning teachers. Motivations and reasons for entering the profession are highlighted. It uses stories from the field to expose some misleading myths and to illustrate key lessons throughout the book. This book is more than just another trip along the often-torturous road of academia. In the following review of the chapters, each myth is followed by a reality check outlining more promising approaches.

Chapter 1. "Myth #1: Don't Smile Until December. Reality: You Need to Smile Early On, and as Often as Possible to Build a Healthy Classroom Climate." This chapter looks at building a positive classroom community while still practicing effective classroom management. The focus is on developing relationships with students.

Chapter 2. "Myth #2: Teaching Is a Cushy Job. Reality: Teaching Is Hard Work and Requires Year-Round Planning in Addition to Daily Preparation and Professional Development." This chapter examines the widespread myth that teachers get a 3-month breather in the summer and are home by 2 P.M. everyday. This chapter looks at teaching as challenging but rewarding work; the hard work is worth it.

Chapter 3. "Myth #3: Good Teachers are Born, not Made. Reality: Teachers are Lifelong Learners Continually Growing in Their Profession from Their "Aha" Moments Through Their Veteran Mentoring Years." We've all heard the statement, "I know everything about the subject, I love kids, I don't need training." Learning to teach is a balancing act, and training is a critical part of keeping your head above water.

Chapter 4. "Myth #4: Good Teachers Don't Make Mistakes. Reality: Good Teachers Learn From Their Most Dramatic Mistakes." This chapter explores the concept of lessons learned from falling flat. The best learning comes when fear is driven out of the classroom.

Chapter 5. "Myth #5: Good Teachers Teach Facts. Reality: Good Teachers Teach the Whole Child How to Think and Learn." Teachers are never off duty. What you drive, what you wear, everything about you is noticed, on campus or off. Teachers need to be authentically enthusiastic for the subject and radiate passion for teaching the whole child. Often the memory of a teacher and the learning that took place has little to do with the information transmitted. It's more a matter of who you are and how you made students feel.

Chapter 6. "Myth #6: They Can't Learn; They Belong in Special Education. Reality: Every Child Can Learn and Is Legally Entitled to the Best Education." This chapter looks at inclusion, and the misguided reluctance to include special education children in the regular classrooms.

Chapter 7. "Myth #7: Teaching Is a Lonely Job. Reality: Teaching Is a Collaborative Profession and Today's Schools Are Professional Learning Communities." This chapter supports working together for a common good. In schools, this means getting along with and involving colleagues, administration, and parents. It looks at the role of leadership in teaching.

Chapter 8. "Myth #8: Teaching Is a Dead-End Job. Reality: The Rewards of Teaching Are Unending." This chapter looks at the rich payback we get as teachers, too often many years down the road.

I hope you find this book a source of inspiration and a powerful connection to what teaching really means. Wherever you are on your path, may it deepen your contribution to your students and help you keep your eye on the profound beauty that is developed by great teachers.

Acknowledgments

My thanks to my editor, Faye Zucker, for her support and faith in me through this project.

I am grateful to the many teachers in my life. Special thanks to those who contributed stories to and inspired ideas for this book: Larry Bailey, John Bartelt, Linda Caputo, Gary Carl, Yvonne Davis, Diane Deal, Larry Deal, Laura Deal-Russi, Virginia Diaz, Dick Gale, Eleanor Graham, Patti Hill, Karen Huigens, Tom McGuire, Lisa Noonan, Emily Shoemaker, and Myrna Wheeler.

I have a large, loving family, many of whom are teachers. Gratitude to all of them for the wonderful role models of what a teacher should be.

Leonard Pellicer provided constant encouragement and expertise. My cousin Terry Deal helped me to say things in the best possible way. I thank you both.

My children and their families are the foundation of my life. I couldn't have done it without you. My sons Jerry and Larry, their spouses Sharon and Kari, and my daughter Donna Nasmyth and her husband Pete provided constant encouragement. My grandchildren Austin, Summer, Camille, Kurtis, Chloe, Kalista, and Karly helped me keep perspective on what teaching is all about.

Publisher's Acknowledgments

Corwin Press would like to thank the following reviewers for their contribution to this work:

Gail McGoogan, NBCT, Narcoossee Community School, Narcoossee, FL

Cathy Lutz, Teacher, Madison Station Elementary School, Madison, MS

Patricia Clark, 1st grade Teacher, Gotham Avenue School, Elmont, NY

Mary Eby, 2nd grade teacher, Woodbine Community Schools, Woodbine, IA

Chris Laster, Teacher, Russell Elementary School, Smyrna, GA

John Pieper, Teacher, Webster Stanley Elementary School, Oshkosh, WI

Pam Roller, Teacher, Galveston Elementary School, Galveston, IN

Carrie Jane Carpenter, Teacher, Deschutes Edge Charter School, Redmond, OR

Marilyn Katzenmeyer, Professional Development Center, Tampa, FL

J. Victor McGuire, University of Nevada, Las Vegas

Debbie Gordon, Teacher, Madison School District, Phoenix, AZ

About the Author

 **Peggy Deal Redman, EdD,** has been an educator for the past forty-five years. Her teaching experience in the public schools has been varied, including middle school math, history, and English; teacher of the gifted from Grades One through Six; and in second and third grades. For the past fourteen years she has been Director of Teacher Education and Professor of Education at the University of La Verne where she has trained thousands of teachers. She received her BA from La Verne College and her MEd and EdD from the University of La Verne.

This book is dedicated to my parents,
Jerry Deal and Edna Brubaker Deal,
two outstanding educators and my first teachers.

1

Myth #1:
Don't Smile
Until December

*Reality: Smile as Early On
and as Often as You Can to
Build a Healthy Classroom Climate*

*Gloom and solemnity are entirely out of place in even the
most rigorous study of an art originally intended to make
glad the heart of man.*

—Ezra Pound

THE MYTH

It took me three years as a neophyte teacher to understand
that students did not have to sit in rows and listen to my
words of wisdom all day. I knew participation was important,
but because of advice from others it was difficult to find my

own voice. I was fortunate to have mentors who encouraged me, but it was here during my early teaching years that I first encountered the myth well known to teachers, "Don't smile until December if you want to maintain control of the classroom." The specific version of the myth I learned advised not smiling until Christmas, but I'm sure other cultural traditions have similar versions of the same myth, repeated over and over by seasoned teachers to the beginner. While it is well-meaning advice from experienced classroom teachers, it doesn't resonate with my observations as a teacher and a teacher of teachers. Behind this myth is the idea that the most important aspect of teaching is maintaining control of the classroom. Control is important, but when students do not have a desire to learn, a healthy classroom climate does not exist.

CARING TEACHERS ARE PART OF YOUR HISTORY

One of the questions students entering our teacher preparation program are asked is "If you think back to teachers who were important mentors in your life, what are the qualities that made them good teachers?" The answers to this question are amazing in their similarity. While candidates often say a teacher's knowledge of the subject matter is important, the one theme that comes through in most responses relates to how much the teacher cared. Examples are cited of teachers who took time to listen to their concerns, ones who saw their struggles and worked to help them achieve, teachers who were available after school and willing to work with them. These are the teachers with heart and passion for their students as well as their subject. These are teachers who care. While many were perceived as strict, you can bet they smiled early and often and certainly before December.

Good teachers care about their students.

Caring is another aspect of maintaining control. It is a delicate balance of demonstrating your authority early and supporting the students with actions that show you care. A healthy classroom climate builds a strong environment for learning.

STUDENTS NEED TO WANT TO LEARN

We as teachers are authorized to teach, we are given the authority, but each student has to sign off on it in order for it to work. Without buy-in from the students in class, a teacher's authority is worthless.

My first teaching job was in an urban junior high school. I was 22 years old, idealistic, and teaching my two favorite subjects, history and math. I was out to change the world. My fifth-period class (right after lunch—always the most difficult time of the day) was an eighth-grade math class, labeled the "Z" group. There were 15 students in the class, many of them taller than I, and, as you have probably guessed, their math skills were lacking. This was a challenge for which I was not prepared. I had always loved math and really didn't comprehend that there were students in eighth grade who couldn't add or subtract. One day we were doing a math problem that required a student to plug in the number of siblings in his or her family to get a predicted outcome. One young man's calculations would not work. We checked the math; it was correct. After careful rechecking we finally discovered that for the problem to work the number of siblings needed to be fewer than ten, and Freddy had fifteen brothers and sisters.

I tell this story because this is where I learned one of the most important lessons of my teaching career. Students do not learn unless they want to learn, and this desire to learn was closely tied to my ability to care about them as human beings. We made progress in the area of math, but where we really made progress was in the way the students felt about themselves. They loved me, and I loved them. They exhibited this love and appreciation in a very tangible way soon after spring break. I was pregnant and had

> *Good teachers develop a community of learners.*

to leave my position as soon as the pregnancy showed (archaic, but true), and this marvelous group of students, who would be classed misfits by many, gave me a party and pooled their resources to present me with a car bed for my first born. I can assure you I smiled before December, and we were a community of learners.

Teachers Open Their Hearts

It is important for a teacher to know the students in his or her class, and to do this, the teacher's heart needs to be open to them. Each student comes with a story, and as the stories unfold, the caring teacher uses the information to help each student attain success, both academically and socially. This thought was brought home to me a few years ago when Parker Palmer was on our campus sharing his learning with us in a faculty workshop. Before meeting with him, each participant was given a copy of Palmer's (1998) book *The Courage to Teach*. This powerful book is filled with insights and examples, but, in his gentle way, Parker brings his stories to life. His book is built on a simple premise: "Good teaching cannot be reduced to technique; good teaching comes from the identity and integrity of the teacher." He shared stories of great teachers in his life. Some were lecturers, others hands-on instructors, yet all created a connectedness and sense of community that is the bread and butter of teaching and learning. I am certain these teachers revealed their hearts to students, certainly smiling before December. The following quote from Palmer's *Courage to Teach* gets at the essence of an effective teacher:

Good teachers have heart.

> Teaching tugs at the heart, opens the heart, even breaks the heart—and the more one loves teaching the more heartbreaking it can be. The courage to teach is the courage to keep one's heart open in those very moments when the heart is asked to hold more than it is able so that teacher and students and subject can be woven into the fabric of community that learning, and living, require. (p. 11)

The Joy of Teacher/Student Reconnection

A good friend of mine, Myrna Wheeler, received an inquiry via the Internet from a former student, Steve, asking if she was the person who taught at a certain middle school in the early 1960s. When she responded with a yes, he was overjoyed to have the opportunity to reconnect with her because of the profound effect she had on him in seventh grade. He recounted coming back into the classroom from lunch and seeing her in the front of the classroom with her head on the desk, crying at the news of President Kennedy's assassination. He identifies this experience as one of the most important moments of his life. He stated, "It was really a gift to me. . . . There is absolutely no doubt that an honest display of emotions is one of the greatest gifts we can give young people. And, ever since that day I have carried with me the idea that, when something bad or sad happens, and one is at a total loss as to what to do, crying isn't a bad choice."

Good teachers are authentic with their students.

Steve went on to obtain his PhD, has been professor, dean, and vice-president at the university level, and does consulting with agencies in the field of community panic (issues such as Columbine, multiple homicide, or child abuse allegations). He is making a difference in the world, and carries to this day the image of his seventh-grade teacher openly expressing her grief over a tragic personal and national loss. She was not afraid to let her emotions show, both joy and sadness.

As teachers, we never know when a word or a deed may be remembered by one of our students. Many years later a former student may tell the teacher, or the story may be passed on through a third party, or we may never know. In the case of Mrs. Wheeler, and her student, Steve, he trusted her, and he reflected, "For a seventh-grade boy, struggling to learn what it meant to be a young man, your tears that day were a revelation. To this day, I am grateful that Mrs. Wheeler was there when we got back from recess, and didn't go outside or to the teachers' lounge or didn't hide her tears." Mrs. Wheeler made a lasting impression on Steve; his emotional growth was promoted by her willingness to be authentic with her feelings. She certainly smiled and cried before December.

Good teachers are remembered.

A Teacher's Legacy Lives On

At our local mini-mart adjacent to the university, one of the managers, Bob, shared a thought with me. He said, "Your mother, Mrs. Deal, was my kindergarten teacher, and I thank her every morning when I get up for teaching me to read." My mother has been gone since 1988, but her legacy is carried on in the lives of the many students she taught. She had a strong sense of discipline in her classroom. Children knew what the expectations were, but she loved them, and they knew it. Bob is just one of thousands of students who were a part of her 35-year career. Three former students from her seventh-grade class, taught in the 1940s, planned and coordinated her retirement party. One is a principal, another is a teacher, and the third played an active role in the education of children at his church. All three are members of the Latino community and were part of the integration of this elementary school in 1952, before *Brown vs. Board of Education*. Each continues the legacy of education modeled by Mrs. Deal.

Relationships Are Critical to Effective Classroom Management

Several years ago, Lee Cantor, the guru of Assertive Discipline, consulted at our university. One of the most significant things he shared was the importance of developing relationships with the students. He emphasized the building of relationships as important for both student achievement and teacher retention. After years of study and practice, he knows that positive teacher/student relationships are a key factor in an environment where learning takes place. I remember a former student in the teacher preparation program relating a practice he used in his classroom. His teaching assignment was at a large, diverse urban high school where he was a biology teacher. He identified the most difficult student in each

Good teachers build relationships with students.

class and made that student his project. He made it a point to give encouragement, create opportunities for success, and most important, to develop a relationship with the student. While it may not have worked in every case, the relationships developed helped give the students a sense of self-efficacy and empowerment that is often missing in a high school student who is struggling.

RESPECT IS ALWAYS PRESENT
IN A LEARNING CLASSROOM

In order for a classroom to function effectively and for learning to take place, it must be managed well. Management of a classroom is more than a set of rules. It is sound instructional planning and delivery. It is establishing good relationships with parents. It is making positive social interaction a priority, helping students to care about each other. It is teaching behaviors—how we transition, how we line up. But in all cases,

Good teachers make respect a key component of their classrooms.

the management of a classroom is the job of the teacher *and* the students. Respect needs to be present, but it is a three-way street: students' respect for the teacher, teacher's respect for the students, and students' respect for one another. Relationships are forged, and an environment established that encourages learning, a true learning community. If this community is to work, the teacher needs to be honest with the class, honest in both words and

Good teachers smile before December.

actions. Teachers, in order to be authentic in who you are and to celebrate the joy of teaching, you MUST smile before December.

If we succeed in giving the love of learning, the learning itself is sure to follow.

—John Lubbock

QUESTIONS FOR REFLECTION

1. What is the kernel of truth behind the myth, "Don't Smile Until December"? Give an example from your experience.

2. What are the benefits of developing a positive relationship with a difficult student?

3. How does developing a community of learners in a classroom enhance learning?

4. What is one way you would show students you have an open heart?

2

Myth #2: Teaching Is a Cushy Job

Reality: Teaching Is Hard Work and Requires Year-Round Planning in Addition to Daily Preparation and Professional Development

Anyone who stops learning is old, whether at twenty or eighty. Anyone who keeps learning stays young. The greatest thing in life is to keep your mind young.
—Henry Ford

THE MYTH

"I wish I had your job. You're finished by 3:00 P.M. every day, and you have the whole summer off." How many times does a teacher hear this statement from friends in other professions? They see teaching as a cushy job, one that requires minimal time on the job, and, by implication, is not nearly as difficult as their daily routines. After decades in the teaching profession, I find this comment interesting, and totally lacking in the understanding of a teacher's daily life.

One of my colleagues suggested we should ask the politicians who legislate on behalf of education to be a "Teacher for a day" or, better yet, a "Teacher for a week." This is an interesting idea, one which could change the direction of education. Time in the classroom is nonstop. Pressure to address standards is ever present. Each student has a special need to be met. This can range from the student who "just doesn't get it" in an eighth-grade algebra class to a third-grade second language learner struggling with reading.

Work doesn't stop at the classroom door. There are papers to grade, lessons to plan, parents to call, all done after the teacher is off the clock. All teachers know that teaching is hard work and requires year-round planning in addition to daily preparation and professional development. Lifelong learning is a given. Teachers need to continue to learn and grow throughout their careers.

Wrapped around this knowledge is the belief of all good teachers that we can make a difference in the life of a child, whether a high school biology student, a brand new kindergartener, or an immigrant youngster who struggles with the English language.

In spite of all this, good teachers share idealism, a belief in the integrity of each student, a commitment to help all children learn. Sometimes it is difficult to keep that idealism alive given the constraints of teaching today. I tell my students to hold on to it, to make it their goal to be as idealistic the day they retire as they are today. It is how teachers connect with students, how they make the world a better place.

Good teachers are idealistic.

TEACHERS ARE HARDWORKING

I know teachers are hardworking. I grew up in a family of teachers. I know it's not a cushy job. My sister-in-law, Diane

Deal, is the poster child for a dedicated teacher. She began as an English teacher in middle school and ended her career teaching kindergarten. She put her whole life into her teaching. As a family we always camped and water-skied at the Colorado River over spring break. I don't remember a trip without Diane spending part of each day doing schoolwork. It began with English essays, and continued with the endless preparation of activities required of all kindergarten teachers. I asked Diane to reflect on the idea that teaching is a cushy job. She responded, "Any job is cushy if you don't care." She went on to reflect about the dedication of teachers. She said, "No job is easy if you give it your all." Students come to us with problems. Good teachers care about the problems of their students.

Good teachers are dedicated.

I know Mrs. Deal was a teacher who lived out what she believed. I remember the response of a young man in a gifted class I was teaching when he found out I was related to her. He said, "She saved my sister. When she entered Mrs. Deal's class she didn't believe in herself. She had difficulty learning. Mrs. Deal cared about her, took time for her. Our family loves Mrs. Deal." This is an unsolicited testimony of a sixth-grade student who recognized the difference an outstanding teacher made in the life of a child and her family.

HIGH SCHOOL TEACHERS HAVE UNIQUE RESPONSIBILITIES

My brother, Larry Deal, began as a teacher, ending his career as a high school counselor. He had many opportunities to talk with students about teachers they liked, ones with whom they signed up to take classes. One observation he shared with me was that students know the teachers who are hardworking and caring. The idea of taking a class for an easy A is another myth. Lazy teachers are not popular with students. Larry talks about a math teacher at Ganesha High School in Pomona who is a favorite of students. She teaches the AP classes, and her students do exceptionally well on the

Good teachers work hard and care.

AP examinations. She makes them work hard, and students appreciate how hard she works. They know she cares. Each semester she teaches one class of remedial math, and she receives the same level of commitment and respect from her students who are struggling with math.

Teachers in high school see up to 150 students per day. Each learner comes with a different background, a specific set of needs, abilities, and hopes. Good teachers work to meet these unique requirements. A friend of mine who is a high school teacher characterizes English teachers as perpetually lop-sided because of the bags of essays they carry around with them. The number of hours spent grading essays is incalculable for these teachers.

Another dimension the high school teacher faces is time spent at school beyond the school day. Effective teachers are involved in the lives of their students. This means assisting with a track meet, teaching the cheerleaders, coaching an athletic team, or advising the yearbook staff. These are only a few of the demands on time for high school teachers. They work hard.

> *Good teachers are involved in the lives of their students.*

KINDERGARTEN TEACHERS MAKE A DIFFERENCE

Kindergarten teachers are my idols. The work they do is endless, and today the standards require a level of learning that is often out of sync with developmental readiness. My mother was a kindergarten teacher for 35 years. One year after the untimely death of my father, my brother and I encouraged our mom to go on a trip. I assured her I would substitute for her during her 2-week absence. I can tell you, I have never worked harder in my life. She had two kindergarten classes, one morning, one afternoon, 32 in each class, with no aide. On top of this impossible situation, it rained every day that she was gone. Believe me, I know how hard kindergarten teachers work. I didn't sit down for two weeks.

I had a personal experience this year with a powerful, caring, committed kindergarten teacher, Karen Huigens. My granddaughter Chloe is in her class. Mrs. Huigens noticed some physical limitations in Chloe. She called her mother and said she may want to consult a doctor. To make a long story short, after trips to UCLA Medical Center, and many tests, Chloe was diagnosed with juvenile rheumatoid arthritis. She has medication, is regularly in physical therapy, and is functioning well in her class. This teacher paid attention to her students. She developed relationships with parents. She made a difference in the life of a child.

> *Good teachers notice their students.*

PROFESSIONAL DEVELOPMENT IS A MUST

Teachers need to be lifelong learners. Professional development is required to keep a credential current. I think this is a powerful part of the job of teaching. Teachers need to keep learning. They need exposure to new ideas. They need to rework old ideas. They need to share ideas that work with their colleagues. When I received my credential, I was eligible for a life credential after five years of successful teaching. This meant I did not have to pay to renew it. I was not required to do any further study. I was as good as I would get. This sounds archaic, but I can't help but think the current requirements for regular, documented professional development grew out of the laziness that some of my colleagues developed toward continued learning. Now teachers in California are required to complete and document 150 hours of professional development every five years. Teachers are constantly learning and renewing the passion they brought to teaching.

> *Good teachers are lifelong learners.*

The Induction Program developed in California is a powerful one. All preliminary teachers are required to work with a mentor for their first two years of teaching. Personal support is given to the neophyte. Professional development opportunities are provided. Experts in the field like Harry Wong and Ruby Payne are brought to the districts to inspire and teach. New teachers work at strengthening the strategies and assessments developed in their teacher education programs. I like building the idea of continued learning into what we do as a teacher. These teachers develop an understanding of the part played by professional development.

SHARING IDEAS

Teachers share what they do. If I develop something I think would work for others, I willingly share it with others. My colleague Linda Caputo tells our students, "Steal anything you can." I like the word "share" better, but she has the right idea. Many professions develop a new idea and protect it so others do not have access.

Good teachers share ideas.

I have witnessed many conversations in the teachers' room where teachers are swapping ideas, papers, even volunteering to run off extra copies for those who like their idea.

New teachers need to be open with their needs. Tell your colleagues if you need something. The worst thing to do is to keep your thoughts to yourself and suffer alone. Teachers are supportive of new teachers and teacher candidates. Don't be afraid to ask.

Teaching is about growing and developing and practicing in situations that are never the same. This is both the joy and the curse of teaching. You will never be bored as a teacher. There is always a new challenge, a new way to do things. With the unique requirements, it is impossible to use the same materials or the same approaches year after year. Practice sharing. When you have a new idea, give it to someone, or ask the person to look it over. He or she may give you a slightly different spin— it becomes better because two people have worked on it together. Bill Ayers (2001) in his book *To Teach* says, "Teaching can still be world-changing work" (p. 8). We need to practice this world-changing work together, sharing our ideas, growing and developing together.

YOU NEED TO TAKE CARE OF YOU

An area of which teachers need to be constantly aware is the need to keep their lives in balance. Because of the demand on your time beyond the classroom you need to constantly work to keep a healthy perspective on life. Once I had a student who was working as an intern during his final phase of student teaching. He landed in the hospital as a result of stress. When he returned to his job we had a heart-to-heart talk. Prior to teaching he had worked for ten years in the entertainment industry. He possessed outstanding skills in film and editing. His school had him working above and beyond his regular job doing projects for the school. Finally he reached his limit, and his health suffered. I talked about his being the only person who could say no. I explained that his colleagues would continue to ask for help; he needed to be the one to say no.

Good teachers take care of themselves.

This example has been helpful to me when I work with students whose passion sometimes carries them beyond their personal limits.

I always tell my student teachers they are to stay at school as long as their master teacher is there. They need to participate in parent conferences, teachers' meetings, and preparation time. I received a call at home one night from a student teacher. She said, "You told me to stay as long as my master teacher did each day. She stays until 8:30 P.M., and I have a young family. I can't do it." From that time on I changed my spiel. I need to work at helping student teachers be responsible, but I need to support the balance in their lives.

In teacher preparation programs, candidates reflect throughout the program. I encourage beginning teachers to continue this practice. They keep a journal during student teaching.

I suggest they keep up this practice, reflecting daily on their professional and personal successes and challenges.

TEACHING IS NOT A CUSHY JOB

Good teachers work hard. A classroom of young people requires constant attention. There is seldom an opportunity to sit down. But at the end of the day, a good teacher has as much to do when he or she goes home. We teach because we believe in the power of all children to learn. We teach because we believe in the strength of an educated populace. We teach because we have a deep passion to help young people learn and grow. Teaching is not a cushy job.

Teaching is not a cushy job.

> *I always tell students that it is what you learn after you know it all that counts.*
> —Harry Truman

QUESTIONS FOR REFLECTION

1. What is the kernel of truth behind the myth, "Teaching Is a Cushy Job"? Tell about a time when you encountered this myth.

2. What are some examples of hard work by teachers? In preparation? Grading papers? After school activities?

3 List opportunities for professional development. How can you expand this list? How can your colleagues help in this area?

4. Discuss ways you can keep your life in balance.

3

Myth #3:
Good Teachers
Are Born, Not Made

*Reality: Teachers Are Lifelong
Learners Continually Growing in Their
Profession From Their "Aha" Moments
Through Their Veteran Mentoring Years*

*Teaching depends on growth and development, and it
is practiced in dynamic situations that are never twice
the same.*

—Bill Ayers

THE MYTH

I have to admit, there have been times when I have made the
statement, "He was born to be a teacher." With that statement

comes the implication that a person is a teacher by nature and needs little to improve practice. Over time I've learned this statement refers to inner characteristics of a person, and assumes that training is an extra. It is impossible to deny that many people have the aptitude and demeanor suited to teaching. They possess the personal attributes necessary for teaching. What this assumption forgets is that teaching is a complex notion, requiring constant work and practice to reach best practices. It takes hard work to succeed.

Today there are those with degrees in hard-to-fill areas that believe all it takes to teach is to go into a classroom and deliver knowledge. Teaching depends on dreams and hopes, but these attributes need to be coupled with skills and knowledge—knowledge above and beyond the subject being taught. The age-old discussion about teaching being an art or a science continues to be on the lips of educators.

TEACHING AS AN ART AND A SCIENCE

My job is the training of teachers. Teacher education faculty need to help students understand the science of teaching while keeping the art alive. A program training teachers is like a quilt, built one patch at a time, but ending with a finished product that is beautiful to behold. Effective instructional strategies that meet the needs of diverse students provide the material for one patch. The special needs student and the second language learner are considered in every lesson planned. They provide the color and pizzazz of the final product. Each lesson adds to the complexity of the quilt, giving it a distinct pattern. Another square represents the teaching of reading and its place in the overall training of the candidate. Phonemic awareness and teaching through texts in the content areas are essential to the coherence of the model. The content knowledge of the teacher candidate is the filling for the quilt. It needs to reach every corner of the masterpiece for the teacher to be complete. This quilt

Good teachers use the science of teaching.

represents the science of teaching, skills, knowledge, and training.

As we survey our quilt, we realize something is missing. It has all of the components of beauty, but is lacking what holds it all together. The stitching of loving hands is the element that represents the art of teaching. Working with a child as an individual is as important as a lesson plan or subject matter competence. When a person is asked to talk about a favorite teacher, the discussion is often summed up with this phrase, "They cared." The stitching on the quilt represents the hopes, dreams, and personal commitment a teacher brings to the classroom. This is the art of teaching. My friend and colleague, Emily Shoemaker, puts it well: "People can't practice the art of teaching until they understand the science of teaching." She would be proud of our quilt, integrating all of the elements of effective teaching.

> *Good teachers are practiced in the art of teaching.*

ALWAYS LOOKING FOR NEW WAYS TO DELIVER

When you visit a school, look for those innovative touches in a classroom. Is there artwork? Is there something the class is working on together? One thing I've learned is that the great teachers are constantly growing. While they may use some information from last year, they are always looking for new ways to deliver. It is such a temptation for neophyte teachers to rely on the Internet, teachers' manuals, and other canned lessons for ideas. I know that the best lessons I ever taught were the lessons developed for a specific class at a specific time. I admit, I often tried the lesson again with the next year's class, but success was never as fruitful as the original effort. The needs of the class are paramount to effectiveness.

One year I was teaching third grade, and we were in the midst of the third quarter doldrums. This is the time before spring break, and June seems a long ways off. Teachers and students know the down feeling of this period. I needed to come up with a strategy to perk up the class. I developed a system of "Redman Bucks." Students were rewarded for turning in homework, finishing work in class, behaving well— all students had an opportunity to earn bucks. I made sure each student was supported, even those who had a more difficult time conforming. The bucks accumulated. Each student developed a system for keeping track of his or her earnings.

Good teachers
are always looking for
new ways to deliver.

At the end of the month, each student tallied the money accumulated. As the banker, I took an accounting of each student's total. It was a great exercise in organization. Careless students paid the price, searching through their desks for crumpled bills. Others had their notes neatly stacked, ready to report numbers. Now it was time to spend our Redman Bucks.

We planned an auction for the next week. Students brought toys they were ready to discard, and I bought items at the 99-cent store to add to the stash. We collected enough for a memorable event. The day of the auction, students were ready. The results were better than I could have imagined. Disadvantaged youngsters bought little-used toys brought in by children from more affluent backgrounds. All of the students went home with something they wanted. As auctioneer, I made sure each child received something of worth to him or her. It was a great day in our classroom. This activity demonstrates both the art and science of teaching.

In my mind, this was an activity developed for this class to meet a specific need. However, younger brothers and sisters wanted to be in Mrs. Redman's class so they could participate in the auction. I continued having auctions, but I admit it was never as successful as the first year when it was designed for a specific class, at a specific time, and for a specific purpose.

Each teacher needs a variety of strategies. These important techniques of teaching need to be honed to meet the needs of the students in your classroom. All teachers need help in this area, and help is close at hand. In elementary school you work with your grade-level team. Many of my best ideas over the years began to germinate as I shared with others teaching the same grade as I. New teachers need to recognize this source and use it as they grow. Middle school and high school teachers work with departments to develop new techniques for delivering content. But don't be afraid to talk to colleagues in other disciplines.

Good teachers use many different strategies.

Some of my best ideas when I was a math teacher came from my collaboration with my colleague who taught history. Working together always makes for better teaching. Don't be afraid to ask.

With strategies in hand, a teacher needs to remember it is real people who are being taught. Whether teens or primary students, it is the human touch that makes the best lesson effective. We need to have a sense of humor, limitless patience, lots of love, and passion for our subject. But most of all, we strive to instill the love of learning in all those

Good teachers remember students are real people.

we teach. This is the greatest gift a teacher can give and the one that demonstrates the true art of teaching.

GROWING THROUGH REFLECTION

As teachers grow in developing the love of learning in their students, they need to be constantly learning about themselves. It is critical to know yourself. You need to be constantly asking yourself questions. What are my strengths? What are my challenges? What could I have done differently to make that lesson more effective?

During our student teaching experience, we require each student to keep a daily journal. Things that worked are recorded. Noted are the areas for improvement. If a lesson bombed, suggestions for revision are listed. Sometimes this reflection is as short as a paragraph a day, but it is done every day. When I make my weekly visits to the classrooms of my student teachers, I review their journals and get a feel for the students' weeks. It is a private conversation between supervisor and student teacher.

Five years ago, before No Child Left Behind, most of our student teachers in California were the teachers of record in their classrooms. I know the journal saved one student. He reflected daily and at length about his frustrations with his job. He was in a large middle school, did not have a mentor, and his principal did not have time to deal with his day-to-day needs. He recorded that one day his students were lined up, and the superintendent of the district spoke harshly to his class about their behavior. This almost sent my student round the bend. You can imagine the fear instilled by this action.

My student had never verbally opened up to me or to our seminar group. The journal gave him an avenue to express himself, and for me to be aware of his fears. I can report that he made it through the year and taught for five years at that school before moving to Northern California. The journal was a critical part of this candidate's development.

I encourage all students to continue keeping a journal as they begin their teaching assignments. It helps them to chronicle their feelings and note strategies and ideas that worked or didn't. Thoughts from the journals need to be shared with peers and coaches for feedback and support. Beginning teachers work daily on the how and the why of teaching. Reflection develops both the art and the science of teaching.

Good teachers reflect on their practice.

No Two Days the Same, No Two Kids the Same

It's interesting in life how there are two faces to so many things. This is true in teaching. We learn the science of teaching. We are tested on strategies. We practice in a real classroom. We develop ways to work with second language learners and special needs students. We are ready to teach.

The first day of teaching we have all our lessons ready. In fact, we have enough information for a week in case we run out of things to do. I remember my first day of teaching third grade. I had spent days preparing a welcoming, supportive classroom. I decided to start with rows so I would have better control. I even seated the students in a boy, girl, boy, girl pattern. I was going to be in charge. We had no sooner completed the flag salute when one boy hit the girl next to him over the head with a book. She had insulted his mother, and he was bound to respond. I had to resolve an issue for which none of my training had prepared me—so much for all of my planning. Later I found out that the two families lived next door to one another and despised one another. They were like the Capulets and the Montagues or the Hatfields and the McCoys. My professors were right about one thing: teaching is different every day.

> *Good teachers are ready for the unexpected.*

I remember another incident with the book-wielding young man whom I'll call José. Later in the year I received a call from a father of one of my students. His son was missing his watch. It had been a present from his grandmother, and it had monetary and personal value to the boy and his family. I had a pretty good idea what may have happened to it, but I was not ready to outright accuse a student. I called José aside and asked him if he would like to help me with a mystery. Jimmy's watch was lost, and I needed a detective to help me find it. José was excited to help. The next day he came up to me and let me know he had spied Jimmy's watch behind some books. He took me to the spot, we found the watch, and face was saved. I never had another problem in that class with personal items disappearing. No two days are the same in a classroom, and no two kids are the same. We need the art of teaching backed by the training necessary for an effective classroom to help us make the right decisions for our charges.

THE HEART AND THE BRAIN OF TEACHING

Teaching is not for the fainthearted. It requires commitment beyond what many people could imagine. It demands the involvement of the whole person. The personal side, the heart and soul of the profession, is a necessity. This part you may have been born with, but it is certainly refined through years of working with children and young adults. It also necessitates the use of brainpower through continued learning and training in the techniques and strategies of teaching. This

Good teachers use their heart and brain.

takes place during inservices, at conferences, through reflection, and through effective peer relationships. The powerful teachers have both. They know how to teach, but they also never forget that it is people they are teaching. Good teachers use both their brain and heart to get to the pinnacle of their profession. Teachers are lifelong learners continually growing in their profession from their "aha" moments through their veteran mentoring years.

> *But it was only the beginning of their education. Working in the trenches day to day helped each of them gradually develop the know-how and wisdom that can only be gained from experience and practice.*
>
> —Lee Bolman and Terry Deal

QUESTIONS FOR REFLECTION

1. What is the kernel of truth behind the myth, "Good Teachers Are Born, Not Made"? Give an example from your experience.

2. Reflect on the concept of teaching as an art and a science. Can you give an example of teaching as an art? As a science?

3. Talk about some ways of using reflection in your teaching practice. Give specifics.

4. How do you prepare for the unexpected things that happen in your classroom?

4

Myth #4: Good Teachers Don't Make Mistakes

Reality: Good Teachers Learn
From Their Most Dramatic Mistakes

There are no secrets to success. It is the result of preparation, hard work, and learning from failure.

—Colin Powell

THE MYTH

One of the most powerful myths in education tells us we cannot fail. If we are to succeed, we need to get it right the first time. Grades support this myth, and one of the most dangerous traps for a teacher is the need to be perfect. Most teachers liked school; in fact, most loved school. As students, we teachers learned how to play the game. We knew how to ace a test, and were rarely humiliated, because we never answered a question unless we knew the answer. We played it safe. Is it any wonder that students in our classes are held to the difficult standard of perfectionism?

I love watching a baby learn to walk. Each child does it differently; the only part that is the same is the ability to stay upright for a number of steps. Have you watched the process? No one spanks a baby because she falls down, but all are excited when she finally gets it right and takes those first consecutive steps. Why then, when we get to school, is it important to strive for perfection, to get it right the first time?

While this myth may hold true for many teachers, when you observe a classroom where mistakes are not just tolerated, but encouraged, you know real learning is taking place. Good teachers learn from their most interesting mistakes, and they preside over classrooms where this is encouraged.

Good teachers are not perfect.

WHAT IS PERFECT?

The image of the perfect person is ubiquitous in our society. Young girls are bombarded with the image of the beautiful female. Princesses are their models, with life always ending with "happily-ever-after." One of my favorite children's stories is Robert Munsch's (2004) classic, *The Paper Bag Princess*. The kingdom of the princess is destroyed by a fire-breathing dragon who toasts her kingdom to a crisp, including all of her clothes. Reduced to wearing a paper bag, she goes on to rescue the practically perfect prince, Ronald. After a daring save, Ronald makes fun of her less-than-perfect attire, and she discovers the prince is not so charming after all. In fact, one of my granddaughter's favorite lines in the book is when she calls Prince Ronald a bum!

The beauty of this story is the power Munsch gives to the princess. She discovers her own power in living happily-ever-after. Her creativity in finding a solution to a difficult situation is a perfect metaphor for teachers who wish to create a sense of student empowerment in their classroom.

Teachers don't have to be perfect. Our students don't either. A colleague of mine, Linda Caputo, shares anecdotes from her fourth-grade classroom with our teacher candidates: "I need to make a safe place for my student, where he can fall flat on his face and get up and try again." She tells of a student who was scared to tell her the truth. She said, "I need to show kids how to take a risk." In your classroom, look for mistakes; let students look for reasons behind their errors. Make this learning move them forward to greater understanding of themselves and the world around them.

> *Good teachers have classrooms that belong to the students.*

TEACHERS SET THE STAGE

Teachers set the stage. Everything in the classroom environment needs to be questioned. When you walk into a classroom, evidence is everywhere pointing to the values of the teacher and students. How do the bulletin boards look? Do they include student work? Does the classroom reflect all students in the classroom? Does it seem too perfect? Can you read the character of the class in what you see?

> *Good teachers admit they don't know.*

Sometimes classrooms seem too perfect. I call it the "Open House Syndrome," teachers competing to have the best looking classroom with little thought to how it affects or is seen by students. One of the best compliments I received from a student happened two days before the end of school. We had stripped the room to be "ready" for checking out on the last day. A student looked at me and said, "Mrs. Redman, this doesn't seem like our class anymore." I never again took down the things that made it our classroom before the last day of school.

Certainly organization is critical in an effective classroom, but as teachers we need to fight against making this too important. This need to be unsullied spills over into teaching practice if we are not careful. Perfectionism may be mistaken for tyranny, over ourselves and our students. Bill Ayers (2001) states it well in his book *To Teach: The Journey of a Teacher:* "Learning requires practice, correction, self-correction" (p. 55).

All teachers want to be right. We feel, as leaders in the classroom, that our position will be challenged if we aren't perfect. Working with student teachers, I encourage the candidates to be brave enough to admit what they don't know. Ask others for help; invite them to be a part of the learning process. This includes students.

THE LOGIC OF ERROR

For many years I used Mike Rose's (1989) book, *Lives on the Boundary: A Moving Account of the Struggles and Achievements of America's Educationally Underprepared,* as a text for our first course in teacher preparation. It is a compelling story of one person's journey through academia, chronicling how lack of exposure and understanding can affect a child's life in school. Perhaps, however, the more important learning in this book is the number of personal examples from Mike's life, showing how teachers and mentors provided his personal bridge to success.

In his book, Rose introduces the term "logic of error," the intelligence of a mistake, what lies behind misinterpretation of information. Sometimes the reasoning behind a wrong answer makes more sense then a correct response.

This concept is not about students coming to class with cavalier attitudes. Instead, it looks at what we require as preparation. As Mike Rose (1989) stated, we must have "a perspective on failure that lays open the logic of error" (p. 238).

This term is something I have taken into the classroom, trying to find ways to make the classroom a safe environment that encourages risk taking; a classroom where answers to questions are encouraged, with enough time given students to respond. In this setting, students are not

Good teachers encourage risk taking.

allowed to laugh at one another; all take responsibility for the other's learning.

CREATING A SAFE LEARNING ENVIRONMENT

One year, early in my career, I started with a second/third-grade combination. After one month, to balance the enrollment in the school, the third graders were given to another teacher, and my class became a straight second-grade class. I got twelve second graders from the other second-grade classrooms. The teachers in the other second grades were my friends and colleagues, but just enough time had passed for each teacher to know the potentially "difficult" children. My new class now had twenty-two boys and eight girls, with more than our share of students who needed regular behavior modification. I knew I had my work cut out for me, but I also knew the importance of creating a place where each student could be himself or herself. In order to do this, students needed to feel open to learn, to make mistakes, and to feel affirmed.

In less than a month, this notion was tested. During the first hour of class, the door opened, and in the doorway stood a mother, her small son, tousle-haired with a wide-eyed, frightened expression, and the principal. We had a new student. My heart stopped. With a teacher's instinct I knew this child could upset the fragile balance I had worked so hard to develop.

I kept my fears under wraps and went to the door, warmly welcoming the boy, Fred. On the spot, I needed to decide where to sit him. In one of those decisions that later turns out to be brilliant, I seated him next to a hard-working girl, Tiffany. One of the joys in teaching is when something works. Fred struggled with organization, and Tiffany helped him organize his desk. When he struggled with something, she would quietly help him. She made him feel a part of our classroom, keeping his mistakes in perspective, celebrating his successes. The class accepted Fred. I learned later from his mother that Fred had witnessed a trau-

Good teachers create a safe learning environment.

matic event as a young child which affected his ability to connect with others. She thanked me and our class for giving Fred an environment where he could grow.

Pairing Students Is an Effective Technique

The connection of Fred and Tiffany was an instinctive response of a teacher who knew her class. Today we use a technique "pair/share," involving two students in an idea. This encourages participation by pairing students, allowing each pair to come up with a response to a given question. This practice encourages participation, and can give rise to unusual interpretations of the question. Students are allowed to speculate and do it within the safety of a pair. Our students need to have multiple occasions to talk about what they are learning and to explore connections or clashes within deeply embedded beliefs. If we really listen to the stories and the reasons behind errors we come to a new understanding of our students. It is through these conversations that teachers learn about all of the classroom participants—including themselves.

Good teachers encourage sharing.

Students Never Forget

In that same classroom I was introduced to Deshawn, a young man I will never forget. He had trouble complying, argued at the drop of a hat, and daily tested my belief in the dignity and respect of each student. He reminded me every day that his first-grade teacher, Mrs. Jones, was his favorite teacher. Of course the implication was that I was not favored with this honor.

Good teachers make mistakes.

Mrs. Jones, a well-respected teacher in the district, taught at a different school, and I knew her well. One day I bumped into her in the market, and I asked, "What did you do to make Deshawn love you so much?" She responded with amazement, "He said that?" She went on to share this story:

It was fifteen minutes before the dismissal bell, and Deshawn was drumming his fingers, jumping up and down, being generally disruptive. Mrs. Jones, at the end of her rope, turned to him and said, "Deshawn, you little shit, sit down!" She said she knew it was wrong, but it just came out. Then she turned and saw a parent standing at the back door. The parent turned, scurried to the office to tell the principal of this conduct. The principal knew the caring, talent, and success of Mrs. Jones. He saw this incident as an example of being at her wit's end. He sat down with her and worked out a behavior plan where Deshawn would come to the office if she felt she was reaching the point of no return.

This is an example of a teacher's mistake becoming a jumping-off point to help a student develop stronger feelings of self-confidence. Deshawn truly loved Mrs. Jones. The story continues—with caring and support in our classroom, this student went on to complete the second grade. For several years he would stop by my room at the end of each day to check in and let me know how things were going. I was now one of Deshawn's favorite teachers.

As teachers we always wonder what happens to our students. I have to admit I always wondered about Deshawn. One day a friend of mine who is a lawyer said, "I met one of your former students the other day, and he has fond memories of the time spent in your second-grade classroom." I asked who the person was, and he responded with Deshawn's name. I asked, "Is he okay?" He said, "Yes, he's a successful young man who still has affection for his teacher."

CELEBRATE MISTAKES

Your job is to help students learn the things that will make them a success in life. It is your job to engage young people, find ways to make learning something they want to do, and encourage risk taking. We need to model learning from our most interesting mistakes.

Teachers come to the classroom with a toolbox of strategies, knowledge, and skills. Take these tools and use them to create an exciting environment where students come ready to face the next big challenges in their lives.

It is stronger and more fruitful to practice humility in the classroom, to admit what you don't know, to invite others to teach you, and to stay close to your own experience. Good teaching requires audacity, but it also demands humility.

—Bill Ayers

QUESTIONS FOR REFLECTION

1. What is the kernel of truth behind the myth "Good Teachers Don't Make Mistakes"? Share a personal experience that demonstrates this myth. It can be from your experience as a student or as a teacher.

2. What is the most difficult academic subject for you? How did you learn this subject? Did you avoid it? Do you accept your mistakes? Do you think it is okay not to do something right the first time?

3. How do you make your classroom a safe place for your students to risk making mistakes?

4. What are some specific practices you could adopt in the classroom that encourage students to risk?

5

Myth #5:
Good Teachers
Teach Facts

*Reality: Good Teachers Teach
the Whole Child How to Think and Learn*

*Whether we're a preschooler or a young teen, a graduat-
ing college senior or a retired person, we human beings all
want to know that we're acceptable, that our being alive
somehow makes a difference in the lives of others."*
—Fred Rogers

THE MYTH

Today the world of teaching is preoccupied with standards and
standardized tests. Are we teaching the facts? Can we be sure
our students can pass the High School Exit Exam? Will our
school measure up when the scores for the standardized tests

are published in the newspaper? Am I meeting the content standards in my classroom? When the principal comes in for a visit, are my standards posted? If questioned, can a student identify the content standard being taught?

Standardized tests and the content standards may measure a narrow band of knowledge, but they are a large part of the teacher's world. Teacher candidates are taught to identify the standard in the lesson plan, post the standard for all to see, and assess to see if the information is learned. In many programs, lessons are scripted to be sure the teacher addresses the information needed. We need to teach the facts, just the facts, ma'am.

Facts are important, but they do not address the needs of the whole child. Many times students learn the facts, but have no idea how to think, how to apply the facts learned. In the workplace, decisions rely on one's ability to think, to think quickly, and to involve others in a decision. Good teachers teach the whole child how to think and learn. Teaching the whole child was the hallmark of Larry Bailey's sixth-grade classroom.

TEACHING THE WHOLE CHILD

Individual respect was the foundation of Mr. Bailey's classroom. Spending time in Room 24 was an enlightening experience for students and parents alike. The class was housed in a former home economics room, a holdover from the previous K-8 configuration. Stoves, ovens, and sewing machines were missing, but the feel of a variety of workstations still existed. Posters with positive themes adorned the room—"You can do it," "Respect begins with you," "Knowledge is power"—creating an atmosphere of hard work accompanied by acceptance, equal access, and a sense of the value of each person. Students represented a spectrum of socioeconomic strata, from poverty to upper middle class. Latino students and students of European descent were almost equally represented. The students and the teacher modeled respect in how they treated one another.

Mr. Bailey moved among students, answering questions and mediating issues that are an integral part of sixth-grade life. His strong sense of ethics permeated his classroom. When former students reflected on their experiences, many of them, now teachers themselves, used words like "responsibility," "respect," "ownership," and "fairness." They talked about the "mirror room," a room near the back of the classroom with floor-to-ceiling mirrors. Left over from the sewing class, this became the thinking room. When a student had a conflict or needed time alone, he or she was sent to the mirror room to "think about things." Students recalled memorizing Lewis Carroll's *Jabberwocky* and Ernest Lawrence Thayer's *Casey at the Bat* to perform for parents and friends at Back to School Night. Even now, if you get a group of Mr. Bailey's former students together they will regale you with Carroll's "Twas brillig, and the slithy toves did gyre and gimble in the wabe." What wonderful memories, what sustained learning.

> *Good teachers develop responsibility for one another in a classroom.*

All members of the class celebrated special events of their fellow students. Together they supported their classmates as they shared about the family Christmas Eve tamale preparation and the sister's *Quincinera,* along with the Bar Mitzvahs and confirmations. In all my years of teaching I have never again encountered a person who created a classroom where students respected, supported, and genuinely liked each other. A former student stated, "Everyone wanted to please him; they didn't want to let him down." A middle school teacher himself, he still found it hard to define the elusive quality that made Mr. Bailey so special.

THE TEACHER SETS THE STAGE FOR ALL LEARNING

Are you thinking this must have been a person who was trained to work with diversity? Someone who has had the benefit of strong multicultural education training? Larry Bailey began teaching before the word "multicultural" was coined. He is a tall, lanky, light-skinned male dressed in a suit and a tie. He is a strong Mormon, has nine offspring of his own, and has adopted three American Indian children. To look at him you might wonder how this apparently straight arrow, buttoned-down individual could so effectively meet the needs of a diverse group of students. Physical appearance often does not provide clues to the power and strength of a great teacher. Mr. Bailey's background gives some insight into his abilities. But on examination of his personal autobiography, his ability as a "master" teacher emerges. It was best stated by a former student: "It was fun in Mr. Bailey's class; he got your attention. Things were not always straight from the book, but, boy, did we learn. We certainly learned from the texts provided, but most of all we learned about people and how to work together." In Mr. Bailey's class, every student was honored. All students felt a responsibility to one another and to their class. Mr. Bailey demanded respect for others and their opinions. This was a classroom where the whole child was taught how to think and learn.

Good teachers know themselves.

WHY DON'T WE JUST LOVE THEM?

My children grew up watching *Mr. Rogers' Neighborhood.* It always amazed me how such a kind, sensitive man could appeal to kids used to the sound bite wizardry of today's entertainment. His death affected all who responded to his question, "Won't you be my neighbor?" Children who are now parents and parents who are now grandparents felt the loss of a friend. Mr. Rogers believed in love and trust: "Love and trust, in the space between what's said and what's heard in our life, can make all the difference in this world" (2003, p. 63).

Of all the professions, teaching is most based on love. Love was present in Mr. Bailey's classroom, along with trust and respect. Mr. Rogers captured the feeling in his quote. He loved the children who made up his viewing audience. It was evident when you watched him. Each child felt he was talking to him or her. And a colleague of mine, Lisa Noonan, shared a powerful story about how love transformed a school assignment she had in Reno, Nevada. The school was located in a part of town where trailer parks were the housing norm, with the majority of students from low socioeconomic families. When she came to the school, the teachers and administration were at their wits' end. Behavior and other problems were horrendous. As the faculty brainstormed ways of addressing the seemingly insurmountable challenges, a teacher in the back of the room ventured a suggestion. She said, "Why don't we just love them?" A simple statement, but it stopped discussion as eyes turned toward the person who spoke. Someone else said, "Why not?" This opened the door for teachers and administrators to think and talk about how this "love" idea would work. They broke it down into steps, first looking at what wasn't working, and then establishing a workable school discipline plan based on Jane Nelson's (1987) *Positive Discipline.* Teachers bought into the new approaches, and suspensions dropped from 175 to 30, with a 75% decrease in playground infractions. Teacher retention soared; a sense of pride enveloped the school. The strong student focus was undergirded by love and consistency. The happy side benefit was higher test scores.

> *Good teachers know love is fundamental to good teaching.*

This school learned that you can't just set a philosophy and expect everyone to fall into line. Teachers, administrators, and staff were brought in and bought in. They owned the ideas. As teachers helped to hire new teachers, they bragged about "their kids." Not only were learning communities developed in each classroom, but the staff itself became a cohesive community, working for positive change. Teachers stayed. They developed camaraderie and pride in their work. What seemed like an impossible task became a success story, spurred by the comment, "Why don't we just love them?" This story is an example of Nel Noddings' (2003) "ethic of caring." The person before us becomes our central concern. Teaching facts is important, but always in the context of the whole child.

COMMUNITIES OF
CARE AND COMPASSION

An outstanding teacher, Mara Sapon-Shevin (1990) sees the primary goal of a teacher as being to create a shared community of care and compassion. The job of educators is to help each student reach his or her full potential. This includes direct instruction, but also creating a place that challenges and supports the diversity of learners that is often a part of our classrooms.

As teachers, we need to remember the importance of dignity in the lives of our students. As a second-grade teacher I had Henry in my class. The year before in first grade he had been caught painting "La Raza" on the bathroom walls. His first-grade teacher and the administration decided to have him sit out recesses and lunchtime in the principal's office for the remainder of the year. I won't debate the wisdom of this disciplinary action, but I decided the most important thing I could do for Henry was make him a part of our class. Learning was difficult for him, and we certainly had our ups and downs. But Henry soon felt like he belonged in Room 6. As a part of the curriculum, the students were to learn the planets in order, and stand in front of the class to recite them. The prize for each was a poster from Pic n' Save. I allowed several weeks, and all students achieved the goal, including Henry.

Good teachers help all students feel they belong.

The epilog to this story occurred three years later. I was teaching at the university, and Henry was in fifth grade. He had some learning issues but was getting help. He was in the speech teacher's office, and he said to her, "I can say the planets in order." She had him recite them, and he did it perfectly. He said, "I learned that in Mrs. Redman's class, and I got a poster for doing it!" It still brings tears to my eyes when I tell the story. Henry felt a sense of belonging in Room 6, and he was open to learning because he wanted to learn.

Teachers Cannot Escape
Personal Values and Beliefs

In our Teacher Education Program students have time for reflection as a regular part of each class. They ponder such questions as: What drew me to teaching? How do I see myself as a teacher? What are my blind spots? An intense examination of personal beliefs and values is necessary for teacher candidates. Who they are will help them to understand students, and their personal experiences will affect what happens in the classroom. Often candidates question whether they can teach in an environment different from the one in which they were raised. I believe caring, well-prepared teachers can make a difference in the lives all students. Sonia Nieto (2003) in *What Keeps Teachers Going?* cites anthropologist Marilyn Dickeman and her groundbreaking work with teacher identities and how their beliefs and practices are shaped. Each teacher teaches who he or she is; values and beliefs come out of personal background and experience. Each teacher needs to be open to new ways of looking at things, new ways of reaching each child in the classroom.

> *Good teachers know their values and beliefs are part of their teaching.*

Teachers Bring Their
Traditions to the Classroom

As a part of our Teacher Preparation Program at the University of La Verne we have an introductory course called "Diversity, Interaction, and the Learning Process." I teach this course. Throughout the semester we look at how our personal autobiographies affect what we bring to the classroom. We do an exercise entitled "Family Search and Research," which gives each teacher candidate an opportunity to share a family tradition with the class. It may be how their parents met, a notorious person in their ancestry, a naming tradition, a favorite recipe, family reunions, or a world event that affected their family. Many candidates assume initially their families are uninteresting. After sharing with others, it is evident how rich and diverse the backgrounds actually are.

In our Bakersfield cohort we have several students whose families came from the Dust Bowl of Oklahoma. They spent time in the camp at Weedpatch, reminiscent of Steinbeck's *Grapes of Wrath*. Many share their Christmas Eve tradition of making tamales, with the assembly line coordinated by their abuela, born and raised in Mexico. Other families immigrated from Eastern Europe or the Middle East, with special recipes as a part of their tradition. And there is always a story of love at first sight, matched by an arranged marriage that has endured. We come away from the evening of sharing with a sense of how diversity adds to our power as teachers. In our diligence to get through required material, we had not taken time to listen to each other's stories prior to that evening. Once a student stood before the class and sang *a cappella* in a gorgeous soprano, "Lift Every Voice and Sing"; there was not a dry eye in the room. Another evening two students were descendents of the Dr. Ross Dog Food inventor. Those of us who remembered the radio jingle sang, "Give him Dr. Ross Dog Food do him a favor, it's got more meat and it's got more flavor . . ." It brought down the house. Teacher candidates celebrate their diverse cultural heritage during this activity.

Good teachers know traditions are important.

TEACHING THE WHOLE CHILD TO THINK AND LEARN

Teachers who make a difference teach the whole child to think and learn. They provide sound instructional strategies, create a healthy classroom environment, care about the students they teach, and reflect on their practices and past experiences. Years later former students not only remember facts they learned, but remember how it felt to be treated

Good teachers teach the whole child.

with love and respect. It is the latter that is essential for a productive, healthy life.

> *One of the beauties of teaching is that there is no limit to what one can learn. Treat people as if they were what they ought to be and you help them become what they are capable of being.*
>
> —Johann Wolfgang Von Goethe

QUESTIONS FOR REFLECTION

1. What is the kernel of truth behind the myth, "Good Teachers Teach Facts"? Give some examples from your observations in the classroom that demonstrate this myth.

2. How can you use the standards-based curriculum in the classroom to help students think and learn? Give specific examples.

3. What specific strategies would you use in the classroom to develop an environment that encourages thinking and learning? How do love and respect fit into a classroom setting?

4. How does reflection help you to be a better teacher? What are some ways you can build reflection into your daily life as a teacher?

6

Myth #6:
They Can't Learn;
They Belong in
Special Education

*Reality: Every Child Can Learn and Is
Legally Entitled to the Best Education*

*Knowledge—like the sky—is never private property. No
teacher has a right to withhold it from anyone who asks
for it. Teaching is the art of sharing.*
                            —Abraham Joshua Heschel

THE MYTH

Not so many years ago, teachers were reluctant to include
children with special needs in their classrooms. Students
with disabilities were seen as a risk to a successful classroom.

Teachers would often, at the first sign of a behavioral or learning problem, want the student to be "tested" so she could be placed in a special class. Many teachers wanted the student out of the classroom, minimizing the disruption for the rest of the students. The implication behind these efforts was often the unspoken, yet widely recognized myth, "They can't learn; they belong in special education."

With the advent of Public Law 94–142 in 1975, the term "least restrictive environment" became part of the education vocabulary. This ensured that students with disabilities must be educated with nondisabled students to the greatest extent possible. The law gave rise to the terms mainstreaming and inclusion. Amendments came in 1997 through the Individuals with Disabilities Education Act (IDEA). This law did several things: made autistic and traumatic brain injury students eligible for special education services, changed the terminology from "handicapped" to "children with disabilities," and added transition services for students 16 years of age or older. Gifted education is another area often overlooked. Differentiation is the name of the game. Each student is to receive the best education possible and spend at least part of the day in a regular education classroom. Regular education teachers now have the daunting challenge and the potential joy of working with children and young adults with disabilities and special gifts.

WE ARE ALL ONE SCHOOL

Increasing interaction between special education and regular education students changes the school environment. There can no longer be a designated area for special education students, separate recesses, or a specific time for lunch. A sense of sensitivity, love, acceptance, and understanding now needs to permeate the school. A model for this cooperation is found at Gladstone Elementary School in the Bonita Unified School District. This school has forged a partnership between regular education and special education students that

Good teachers work for the good of all students.

can serve as an exemplar for other schools. It has put inclusion and acceptance into practice.

Each year, special education teachers have a regular place on the staff meeting agenda. They talk about students in their classes, focusing on the positive areas and limitations. Special students become known to the regular education staff. This gives both special education and regular education teachers a chance to work hard to create a positive learning environment. Special education teachers also attend grade-level meetings to discuss specific students and their needs. These practices alert regular teachers to the unique issues of including special children into their classes. Finally, special education teachers visit classes where their students are included. They personalize the experience, giving the regular class an opportunity to learn about the special needs of the child who is to become a part of their classroom community. Fourth, fifth, and sixth grades participate in an assembly that highlights scenarios of children with disabilities working successfully in regular classrooms.

Regular and special education students at Gladstone participate in assemblies together, join one another on field trips, share recesses, have the same lunch schedule, are part of the citizenship award program, and enjoy the physical education program together. The buddy program with the fifth-grade students is another example of cooperation. Buddies come into special education classes to read, do art projects, or share their special skills.

Special education and regular education teachers work together.

Special education students are an integral and welcome part of the school. They are given equal opportunities to grow and learn. Another hallmark of the program is the close relationship between the regular and special education teachers. Both are part of every staff meeting and enjoy social events together. A special education teacher is on recess duty each day to monitor and support situations that may arise on the playground. Everyone takes the special challenges seriously. They are committed to providing the best education for all students at Gladstone irrespective of their unique individual situations.

CLASSROOM RISKS OF AT-RISK STUDENTS

Donna Walker Tileston (2004) has written a helpful book, *What Every Teacher Should Know About Special Learners.* In this book she defines the at-risk students as "those students who, without intervention, are a high risk for failure" (p. 21). Criteria for at-risk students could include poverty, past failure, chronic illness, and a host of possibilities. These students are not identified or eligible for a special education program. They are legally part of a regular classroom. Schools across California have School Study Teams (SST). These teams include teachers, the principal, the school psychologist, and others as needed. This is where teacher turns when he or she has a difficult student.

The team meets with the teacher, examines available information, and recommends interventions to meet the student's needs. If, after a month, the new approaches are not proving helpful, the SST is again consulted, and they may recommend further intervention or testing. At the appropriate time, parents join the team. The SST helps at-risk students avoid falling through the cracks. If a school does not have such a team, something else is needed to provide a place for a teacher to go for help.

Good teachers recognize the need for interventions.

Interventions need to begin early; for example, teachers need to aware of the first grader who is not reading by the end of the year. Interventions may not always involve new classroom strategies. They may be as simple as getting a student's eyes or ears checked—or finding out what's going on at home.

DIFFERENTIATION IS THE KEY

As teachers, we need to learn as much about differentiated instruction as possible. There is a wonderful quote by Steven Covey (1990) that highlights the importance of teaching one child at a time,

As a teacher as well as parent I have found that the key to the ninety-nine is the one—particularly the one who is testing the patience and good humor of the many. It is the love and the discipline of the one student, the one child that communicates the love for the others. It's how you treat the one that reveals how you regard the ninety-nine, because everyone is ultimately a one. (p. 197)

This truth demands that a teacher meets the needs of each individual. Diversity in abilities makes differentiated instruction a necessity. It pays off across the board. Students who are engaged and feeling successful rarely demonstrate behavior problems.

Good teachers differentiate instruction.

No Child Left Behind (NCLB) and the standards movement do not require standardization of students' ways of understanding material. Instructional styles need to be flexible in helping all students measure up. A fourth-grade teacher talked about moving away from the classic "California Mission Project," a required staple in the California schools for decades. At its height, missions were designed by architect fathers or engineer mothers, and the whole family built the project. It became so commercialized that mission kits are available at the local Wal-Mart or Target. Recognizing that homogeneity had given way to diversity, students in her class do not have to build a mission. They can choose from a variety of options. They put together a PowerPoint, make a video, develop a travel brochure, write a research paper—or build the traditional mission. This is an excellent example of a required assignment that gives students choice in fulfilling the objective. It meets the needs of the learning disabled and the gifted child.

Good teachers give students choices.

ASPERGER'S SYNDROME

Asperger's Syndrome is a phenomenon more and more common in classrooms. Asperger's is a form of high functioning autism. In many cases, students with this disability are fully included in a regular education classroom. Because of lower social skills evident in this disability, other students in the classroom need to be brought into the picture. A second-grade teacher, Virginia Diaz, brings the parents into the class to talk about the disability's symptoms. She may also invite a special education teacher to share some of the most common behaviors. Virginia finds that students are open to being supportive when they know what's going on and what they can do to help. They become part of the solution, not the problem.

Good teachers help the class understand.

In our teacher education program, students participate in a series of scenarios looking at a variety of ways students can differ. One night, after the presentation of the Asperger's Scenario, a student spoke up. She said, "Many of you were laughing when the scenario was being presented, but I can tell you it's not funny. My brother is an adult with Asperger's, and social skills are still a problem." That night we learned more about working with students with Asperger's than any objective research could have told us.

GIFTED EDUCATION

I taught gifted students, Grades One through Six, for seven years in what we then called a pullout program. When people heard about my "plush" assignment they would be envious. What was hard for them to understand was that it was probably my most difficult teaching assignment. Gifted students are often seen as bright, competent, high scorers on standardized tests. We don't realize that they also have unique needs.

My students ran the gamut. One was the soon-to-become valedictorian who collapsed if a B appeared on her report card. Another was a sixth-grade student organizing a protest against the noon aides at his elementary school. A third appeared to be sleeping in the back row, yet always had the ready answer to the tough question. He went on to graduate from continuation high school before entering college. I learned with this wonderful bunch of students that giving them more work to do would not do. That is punishment, not gifted education. Wiggins and McTighe (1998) say the indicators of real understanding are students who are able to give thoughtful reasons based on evidence and knowledge, students who are able to explain difficult concepts using powerful mental models. I saw this phenomenon every day in my work with the gifted.

Good teachers differentiate for gifted instruction.

This intelligent definition was manifested daily in my gifted classes. Students produced radio programs with commercials and sound effects. They brought Barbies and wrapped them as mummies when King Tut came to town. Some students developed logic problems and used them as challenges for the whole class. An ongoing chess tournament was a daily occurrence. Silk screening was an option. Regular field trips took us to Cal Tech, the UCLA Japanese Gardens, Huntington Gardens, and Kern Foods Processing Plant.

Some students performing poorly in their regular classrooms excelled in the gifted classroom. At the time, no special curriculum existed. I went to every available workshop and conference. I met other teachers of the gifted for lunch. It was a constant search for qualitatively different instruction materials and practices.

The challenge we have today is providing instruction for gifted students within the context of the regular classroom. Not just more of the same, but raising the bar, challenging them on higher levels of Bloom's Taxonomy, and requiring a more complex product. Another strategy would be to develop peer-mediated teaching arrangements. Engagement with others requires higher order thinking skills as students organize materials, develop interpersonal leadership skills, and, most important, develop a tolerance for others' levels of understanding.

ALL STUDENTS COUNT

Effective schools provide for all children, children with disabilities, children with special gifts, and children who have

Good teachers make school a place where all children belong.

problems conforming. An inclusive school provides a way of life that provides unlimited opportunities for students to live and work together. It is a school based on the belief that each individual belongs and is valued. It is a community of learners where all children can risk and grow with the support of other students, teachers, administrators, and parents.

> *There is only one child in the world and that child's name is ALL children.*
>
> —Carl Sandburg

QUESTIONS FOR REFLECTION

1. What is the kernel of truth behind the myth, "They Can't Learn; They Belong in Special Education"? Tell about a time you've seen this myth in practice.

2. What are some of the challenges a regular education teacher faces when a child with disabilities is placed in his or her classroom?

3. List some examples of differentiation for a child with Asperger's Syndrome. What are some strategies that could be used with gifted students?

4. Give examples of interventions that could be used with a student who continually acts out in class.

7

Myth #7:
Teaching
Is a Lonely Job

Reality: Teaching Is a Collaborative Profession, and Today's Schools Are Professional Learning Communities

Without question, teachers are the best and most abundant source of leadership available to schools. Teacher leaders remain the last best hope for significantly improving American education.
   —Leonard O. Pellicer and Loren W. Anderson

THE MYTH

When I began teaching, it was all about my students and me. Each morning, after greeting each child, I would close the door, and it was our private domain. I was it for all the students.

I don't remember students being pulled for speech classes or any other special needs. I was virtually on my own. We had weekly teachers' meetings, but these centered on issues of policy and general school and district issues. As a new teacher, I had little sense of collaboration with colleagues. As a middle school teacher, I was reminded of one connection: we shared students. Students were very open about sharing how another teacher did or didn't do things. Teaching was then a lonely job, stranded among little people, without much adult contact.

EFFECTIVE TEACHING IS COMPLEX

This myth of the isolated teacher continues today, even though the reality our contemporary teacher candidates enter is vastly different from those early memories. When I am observing a student teacher, it is not uncommon for a classroom to have a multitude of interruptions: Johnny is called out for speech, Jennifer goes with the resource specialist to work on her math skills, and Jorge works one-on-one with the Reading Recovery teacher, all this in the space of an hour. Add to that the advent of technology: cell phones, pagers, laptop computers, e-mail, teacher and class Web sites—all providing immediate access to information. These changes put pressure on schools to keep up in a fast-changing, fast-paced world. It's too complex for any teacher to handle alone. Yet we perpetuate the myth of "Teaching is a lonely job."

COLLABORATION IS ESSENTIAL TO GOOD TEACHING

Most teacher education programs focus on subject matter competence, lesson planning, and classroom management. We do not give adequate time to the importance of collaboration among teachers. As teachers enter the profession, they have little feel for the broader vision of transforming schools into learning communities. If they are to have the maximum effect on students in the school and the teaching profession as a whole, they need to exercise leadership. For many years we used a book by Bolman and Deal (1994), *Becoming a Teacher Leader*, to help our candidates understand the importance of leadership in schools. The importance of teachers' understanding the nature and complexity of leadership in the teaching profession is highlighted throughout the book.

> *Good teachers transform schools.*

Bolman and Deal state, "What they don't teach in teacher education is how to broaden your vision, how to sense the deeper social dynamics in your classroom and your school, and how to work with others to transform schools from the isolating and under rewarding environments that they so often become" (pp. 4, 5).

LEARNING COMMUNITIES
SUPPORT TEACHER LEADERSHIP

Teacher candidates need to understand that the school is the place where a teacher develops. The teacher's intrinsic value system and vision for growth are supported and developed within this learning community. Hord (1997) addresses the issue of shared values and vision, connecting them to the learning community. This leads to "binding norms of behavior that the staff supports" (p. 3). The school is a powerful place for a teacher to learn, adapt, and embrace the idea of change.

Sergiovanni (2001) sees schools as places where people are tied together by common, basic values, values that lead to "commitment to both individual rights and shared responsibilities" (p. 88). It is essential for effective schools to operate as learning communities where desired values are identified and made a part of the structure of the way things are done. These values become a part of the school, whether developed as part of a vision statement or a list of tenets. In the complex world of teaching today teachers are empowered to contribute to the values and vision that are a part of the school.

DuFour (1999) puts the principal in the picture as the person who provides teachers with relevant background skills and research findings. Opportunities are provided for training and coaching along with time for reflection and discussion. A true learning community is a team where administration and teachers work together to provide a safe and supportive environment for the students.

TEACHER LEADERS ARE EXCELLENT CLASSROOM TEACHERS

Marilyn Katzenmeyer and Gayle Moller (2001), in their book *Awakening the Sleeping Giant,* confirm the fact that a prerequisite of becoming a teacher leader is to be an excellent classroom teacher. Their definition of teacher leadership is the following:

> Teachers who are leaders lead within and beyond the classroom, identify with and contribute to a community of teacher learners and leaders, and influence others toward improved educational practice. (p. 5)

One of the powerful outcomes of leadership in the classroom is helping to develop future leaders. The teacher models leadership behaviors to students in the classroom. Though it's difficult to imagine as you are working with a group of fourth graders that they will go on to provide leadership for coming generations, it is true. One day about six years ago, I saw the mother of one of my former students at the grocery store. I asked about her son, Dana, who I had taught as a fourth grader in the gifted program. It had been sixteen years since I had her son, but I remembered his thirst for learning. The story she shared was poignant and humbling, and underscores the influence we may have as teachers, even when we don't know it. She shared that Dana had graduated from Harvey Mudd College and was currently a PhD candidate at Cal Tech. She reminded me of the Chess Tournament I had organized in the gifted class. Even though I am a total novice at the game of chess, I taught the students the basic moves than set up a tournament for competition. Dana had never played chess before, but he took to it like a duck to water. He became the champion of our class. But the story doesn't end there.

He fell in love with chess and entered a chess tournament where he won a book about chess. After studying, he entered more tournaments where he won substantial monetary prizes with his prowess. To make a long story short, the money earned from these tournaments helped pay his way through Harvey Mudd College. Through leadership, we affect the lives of those we teach. In many cases we will never know just how. I'm glad I bumped into Dana's mother that day. It helped validate my own passion for teaching.

Good teachers model leadership.

After the advent of collective bargaining, I worked with many schools in our district on issues relating to teachers. This was before the term "teacher leadership" was developed, but I saw it in action without giving it a label. A colleague of mine, Dick, was a history teacher at the local high school. I only knew him through collaborative efforts of teachers representing other schools in the district. One day, while talking to a parent from Dick's school, I learned of his powerful teaching practices. The parent gave example upon example of providing strong subject matter and inspiring students to do their best work. This was the first time I began to understand the concept, combining superior teaching leadership with outstanding classroom practices. Dick was a true teacher leader.

Good teachers collaborate and have sound classroom practices.

A CENTER FOR TEACHER LEADERSHIP

With the advent of shared governance, the need for teachers to take on leadership roles has grown. The University of La Verne saw the need, and under the guidance of Dr. Tom McGuire, chair of the Education Department, the Center for Teacher

Leadership was born. Teachers from local schools who are recommended by a principal, a colleague, and a district office administrator are invited to apply for a summer workshop.

Good teachers are validated at ULV's Center for Teacher Leadership.

Participants attend the workshop which emphasizes personal growth, collaboration skills, and leadership development. Outstanding presenters are the focus of the week. Marilyn Tabor trains participants in Cognitive Coaching. Terry Deal shares thoughts and practical applications of the frames of leadership. Leonard Pellicer works with the group on balancing the power and responsibility of leadership. Tom Harvey guides the group through the processes of change. Networking across schools and districts provides participants with opportunities to learn from one another.

Participants receive literature on leadership (many books written or recommended by the presenters), plus a stipend to take back to effect a change at their respective school sites. Each person receives a crystal apple during the last session with the directions to share the apple with a teacher who made a difference in his or her life. Each is asked to personally present the apple to the teacher, and to share with the recipient the influence the teacher had on his or her life.

Crystal Apples Symbolize Good Teaching

At the three follow-up sessions, teachers share their stories of crystal apple presentations. These stories have a powerful

Good teachers are recognized with crystal apples.

impact both on the teachers receiving the apple and the presenter. One participant gave the apple to her second-grade teacher. She invited the teacher to the culminating luncheon to make the presentation. It was a powerful testimony to the influence of a primary teacher on the practice of an emerging teacher leader. More than a few tears were shed among those at the luncheon.

Another participant went to the class of her college professor and presented the apple in front of a current class of students. The workshop convener, Tom McGuire, gave his apple to his doctoral dissertation chair at UCLA. He shared the experience of making an appointment to have lunch with her. Over lunch he presented the apple, and thanked her for her role in his success. This renowned college professor was moved to tears. She told Tom this was the first such recognition she had received.

Good teachers need validation.

This practice continues with each new group of teacher leaders. As a result of this experience, I urge the students in my classes to identify teachers who made a difference to them and to make every effort to contact them to share their appreciation in person. It empowers each of us when our professional efforts are identified and supported in a tangible way.

At the culminating luncheon, the strongest thread was the power of validation, of being treated as a leader and as a valued member of the teaching profession. Participants have gone back to their respective schools, but periodic reunions validate efforts of a group of strong teachers who are continuing to contribute to their profession.

GOOD TEACHERS EXERCISE LEADERSHIP BEYOND THE CLASSROOM

Recently I received a call from a former student who is now teaching math at a local high school. He is an outstanding teacher. He is viewed as a powerful player in his school, assuming key leadership roles, making decisions that affect the entire school. He has been appointed to a high-level policy committee in the state of California looking at the roles of the principal and teacher. He is on loan from the school district for a year. The concern he registered in his call to me was to be sure the teacher is recognized

Good teachers are recognized at their schools and beyond.

in the leadership equation, and how that might best be accomplished. This is a critical question, and one not often raised when business and administrative people look at school leadership. In order for schools to function at their highest level, teachers must exercise leadership both in and out of the classroom, and their efforts must be recognized and rewarded.

SHARING POWER STRENGTHENS AN ORGANIZATION

These teacher leaders are living proof that sharing power helps to build a team spirit which can strengthen an organization. Leonard Pellicer and Loren Anderson (1995), in *A Handbook for Teacher Leaders*, identify the sharing of power and responsibility as a building block for teacher leaders. They state, "The appropriate sharing of power will frequently result in a team synergy that far exceeds the capabilities of a collection of individuals to contribute to the good of the organization" (p. 39). Teacher leaders have the responsibility to turn followers into leaders, expanding the school wide potential for leadership that can make a difference.

MENTORS HELP NEW TEACHERS

One of the biggest obstacles to effectively integrating teachers into the leadership structure of schools is the inability to find adequate released time in the school day. There is little extra time for teachers to assume the challenge of new roles.

California is in the midst of major reform in teacher education through SB2042 legislation. As a part of the required restructuring, teacher candidates are placed on a

Good teachers become support providers.

sequence beginning with subject matter preparation, moving to teacher training, and culminating with an induction program into the first two years of contracted teaching. One of the important outcomes in the area of teacher leadership is the development of mentors as a part of the induction program at the local school sites. These are classroom teachers carefully selected by their districts to shepherd the new teachers into the fold. Mentors are given released time and a stipend but, more important, are recognized and validated for their roles as leaders of teachers.

GOOD TEACHERS WORK TOGETHER

To be successful in today's world, teachers need to rid themselves of the mythical sense of classroom as kingdom that was, for many years, an accepted part of the teaching profession. Teachers need to reach out and become collaborators, supporters of one another and of the school as a whole. We need to develop skills of teacher leaders to end the isolation that can stunt professional learning and development.

> *Good teachers know that teaching is no longer a lonely job.*

> *What distinguishes leadership from other kinds of relationships is that, when it works well, it enables people to collaborate in the service of shared visions, values, and missions. At their best, teachers, like other leaders, shape relationships that make a measurable difference in others' lives, even though those differences may be hard to assess and may not come to fruition for years after the fact.*
> —Lee Bolman and Terry Deal

QUESTIONS FOR REFLECTION

1. What is the kernel of truth behind the myth, "Teaching Is a Lonely Job"? Give an example of this you have observed.

2. What is one way collaborating with fellow teachers can bring rebirth and new growth to the solitary classroom?

3. How would working with a seasoned teacher give you insights into your everyday application in the classroom?

4. Have you ever seen yourself as an agent of change? How?

8

Myth #8:
Teaching Is a
Dead-End Job

Reality: The Rewards
of Teaching Are Unending

All great stories start with a teacher. All great stories end
with their ongoing influence.

—Mike Rich

THE MYTH

Those outside the profession confront teachers with state-
ments like, "I don't know how you do it!" and "The pay is so
low; why do you stick with it?" Perceptions of teaching as
unrewarding are common among lay people. Their negative
assessments often originate from their own time as students
or their experiences with their own children and teenagers.

I believe, along with friends and family who are educators, that teaching is the best profession in the world! I know teach-

Good teachers are remembered.

ing is rewarding. Students come back and confirm how I have affected their lives. What a thrill for a teacher to learn that he or she has made a difference. Many times former students surpass the teacher in level of education, status, or economic success. Yet they always remember and cherish lessons learned from that special teacher.

A STUDENT REMEMBERS AND CONTACTS A FORMER TEACHER

The Internet helps students find teachers from their past. A longtime friend and colleague, Gary Carl, shared a story of how he was discovered by a former pupil. Gary spent the bulk of his career as a history teacher at San Luis Obispo High School in California. Early in his career he taught and coached at Garey High School in Pomona. Gary loves his subject, and he is appreciated as someone who knows what he's talking about. In a university course of mine, I asked the students to share a story about a teacher who made a real difference in their lives. One of the young women talked about a Mr. Carl in San Luis Obispo. Imagine her surprise when I shared that Gary's family and mine had taken vacations together when we were kids. I had even introduced Gary to his wife of forty-seven years. My student talked about Gary's knowledge, but also about his character and what his example meant to her.

While I was having lunch with Gary and his wife, Anne, several months ago, Gary talked about a postcard he'd received. It was addressed to him, and the message asked

Good teachers help people.

whether he was the Gary Carl who taught at Garey High School in Pomona in the early 1960s. The writer left a phone number, and Gary called. She was delighted to hear from him. She was now a teacher herself, and wanted to thank him for something he had done for her many years ago. In her senior year this student was married, and her husband was in the military. He was to be shipped out midway through her senior year, and she wanted to go along. She talked to Mr. Carl about combining her first- and second-semester government classes into one semester. He recognized her passion and commitment; and worked to make it possible for her to do two semesters in one. She completed the work, and was able to join her husband.

The student wanted to get in touch with Mr. Carl to thank him, but she had no idea how. She was now living in the South and did not know if he was still in Pomona. She did an Internet search and came up with addresses for thirty-two Gary Carls in the United States. She wrote postcards to all 32 with the same query until receiving a response from the right one. So much for teaching being unrewarding.

TEACHERS INFLUENCE THROUGHOUT LIFE

While, as teachers, we know we make a difference, it is easy to lose our calling in the sometimes overwhelming frustrations of day-to-day responsibilities. We lose sight of the real purpose of teaching. In my teacher training class at the University of La Verne, we do an exercise early in the semester asking each student to share a hero in his or her life. Many times the people named are teachers who challenged them, made them believe in themselves, or who showed them undreamed of possibilities. I encourage them to find a way to contact that teacher and recognize the powerful influence that shaped their lives.

One day I was interviewing a young man for our university program, and I left my office to make some copies. When I returned he asked if the person in the picture on my desk was my son. I said, "Yes, did you know him?" He recalled that Mr. Redman was his favorite teacher in the fifth grade. Until that

Good teachers are role models.

time, he didn't realize men could be teachers. This competent young man is ready to enter the profession. A young male teacher in his past helped set him on that path. Sometimes we learn directly of our influence. More often than not it goes unrecognized.

TEACHERS ARE REMEMBERED

A colleague of mine, Patti Hill, has been teaching for thirty-six years, mostly at the middle school level. She is another teacher who stands out. I have been in restaurants with Patti when we receive complimentary drinks from someone at another table who has fond memories of her as a teacher. One of her favorite stories is about a student, Michael, who was in her fifth-grade class. He had recently moved to the United States from England. Michael was a character, a little out of sync with his classmates. One of the things that endeared him to his class-mates was he knew most of the English pub songs.

Michael had a special relationship with Miss Hill, and he called her "Toots"! The other teachers admonished her for the familiarity, but Patti knew Michael needed the special touch of a caring teacher. He never used "Toots" in the classroom, but outside it gave him a unique connection. Michael moved on to middle school where he again had a difficult time fitting in. Yet, lucky for him, Miss Hill was reassigned to the middle school. He still called her "Toots," and he again found her room a place where he could be himself.

When Michael went to high school he still struggled to fit in, and he made many trips back to Miss Hill's *Good teachers* classroom to seek her wisdom. He finally gradu-*build special* ated with little idea of what he would do. Patti *relationships.* received a call from him several years later; he had finally decided he wanted to become a nurse. Time passed without contact with Michael.

One day during fifth period, Mrs. Hill received a call from the front office. There was an important phone call for her, and the principal would be down to take her class. You can imagine what went through her head: is it a parent? Is it a problem? When she arrived at the front office the secretary directed her to take the call in the principal's office. Now the questions were really spinning in her head.

When she picked up the phone a voice said, "Hi, Toots."

She replied, "Michael, what are you doing?" He told her about his job as a nurse on an AIDS ward.

"My patients love me, and I love them!"

Patti asked, "Why did you call me today?"

He said, "I had to call you today, it's your birthday!"

This is another example of the real rewards of teaching.

LEARNING TO READ

Teachers in the early grades are first and foremost teachers of reading. They know students best learn to read through a variety of approaches. When I asked about teaching reading, my niece Laura, a first-grade teacher, shared the multiple strategies she uses. By the end of the year, all her children are reading. Students benefit by exposure to the richness of literature in a variety of genres, yet still need phonemic awareness and phonics to round out the picture.

In the second grade, reading is a designated time of the day. By then most students have developed their reading skills and are reading at grade level. However, sometimes there is a block or an undiagnosed learning disability that surfaces, making reading a struggle. In one of my second-grade classes, I had a student named Sheri. She could not read. In spite of efforts by her teachers in kindergarten and first grade, it hadn't clicked. She found herself struggling with even the simplest of text. Sheri was diligent; she wanted to learn. She did

Good teachers support student learning.

everything I asked of her, and, by the end of the second grade, she was a reader! You could not have had a prouder child, or a more appreciative mother and father.

Over the years, I lost track of Sheri. She had moved away, and I didn't know what had become of her—until I ran into her when she was in her early 20s. She had just graduated from college and had been accepted to graduate school. She was a budding scholar, preparing to eventually become a teacher herself. When I went home that night, I reflected on readiness to read, and the importance of providing a supportive, encouraging environment along with effective instructional strategies. I thought about the power of being a teacher, about what it means to make a difference in someone's life. It would have been so easy to give up on Sheri. I'm so glad I didn't.

TEACHERS HELP YOU GROW

Students often ask me to share a story about one of my teachers who was significant in my life. I share the story of my eighth-grade math teacher, Mrs. Piculell. Math was always my best subject. I would finish the assignments quickly, and then go about the more important work of adolescence—socializing with my friends! This pattern continued until I received a "pink slip" from Mrs. Piculell. This was the equivalent of detention, and it was the first time I been reprimanded in this way. I came in after school, and Mrs. Piculell was waiting for me. I will never forget that conversation. She didn't yell at me or give me a punishment. She just shared how disappointed she was in me. She said, "You have great leadership potential, but if you continue on this path you will never have an opportunity to use it!" My bubble was burst, but it made me think and work at changing some of my habits. The next year I was elected student body president of my junior high school, the first girl to be elected to that position. I still sometimes talk too much, but I will thank Mrs. Piculell for the rest of my life for setting me on a promising leadership path.

Good teachers promote growth.

TEACHING IS REWARDING

As teachers we do make a difference. When a former student lets us know, it makes all the frustrations of day-to-day teaching melt away. So many times I have been told, "I remember what our third-grade classroom looked like." "I remember how you talked to us." "I remember how you made me feel." "I remember the special project we did in the gifted classroom." What an awesome responsibility we have as teachers, and who says teaching does not reap rewards? A quote from Larry L. Leathers in Canfield and Hansen's (2001) *Chicken Soup for the Teacher's Soul* talks about his first year of teaching. He struggled with a group of twelve senior boys who could not graduate because they were minus a credit in science. As a rookie he almost quit. He felt he was incapable of reaching the young men. Two years later, one of the members of that same class met him.

Good teachers are rewarded.

Leathers was taken aback when he said, "Sir, did you ever know that you were our favorite teacher, and your class was our favorite class?"

Leathers replied, "I almost quit teaching because I failed you. So how can you say that?"

"But, Sir, you were the only teacher in high school who cared enough to keep trying, and you never gave up on us." (p. 142)

Teaching is rewarding. Its power can move you to tears.

The sign of a great teacher is that the accomplishments of his students exceed his own.

—Aristotle

QUESTIONS FOR REFLECTION

1. What is the kernel of truth behind the myth, "Teaching Is a Dead-End Job"?

2. Share about a teacher in your life that made a difference to you. What are some of the specific things you remember about that teacher?

3. Fold a piece of paper in half. On the right-hand side list the rewarding things about teaching, and on the left-hand side list some of the aspects of teaching that may be unrewarding. Discuss your list with other teachers or prospective teachers.

4. Think about your own practice as a teacher. What do you think students will remember about you?

Afterword

Writing this book renewed my belief in the power of the teacher. Our teaching today may be framed by external pressures, with standards-based teaching, API scores, and schools being judged by standardized test results, but at the heart of each school are the teachers. With solid preparation surrounded by the desire to do the best for each student, teachers are the hope for our educational system. Teachers bring their hearts and a sense of adventure to the classroom. In partnership with students, they embark on the journey of life, a journey that makes the world a better place. I'm proud to be a teacher.

References

Ayers, W. (2001). *To teach: The journey of a teacher.* New York: Teachers College Press.

Bolman, L. G., & Deal, T. E. (1994). *Becoming a teacher leader: From isolation to collaboration.* Thousand Oaks, CA: Corwin Press.

Canfield, J., & Hansen, M. V. (2001). *Chicken soup for the teacher's soul.* Deerfield Beach, FL: Health Communications.

Covey, S. (1990). *The seven habits of highly successful people.* New York: Simon & Schuster.

DuFour, R. (1999). Help wanted: Principals who can lead professional learning communities. *National Association of Secondary School Principals, NASSP Bulletin.* 83(604), 12–17.

Hord. S. (1997). Professional learning communities: What are they and why are they important? *Issues About Change,* 6(1), 1–8.

Katzenmeyer, M,. & Moller, G. (2001). *Awakening the sleeping giant.* (2nd ed.). Thousand Oaks, CA: Corwin Press.

Kidder, T. (1989). *Among schoolchildren.* New York. Perennial.

Munsch, R. (2004). *The paper bag princess.* New York: Annick Press.

Nelson, J. (1987). *Positive discipline.* New York: Ballantine Books.

Nieto, S. (2003). *What keeps teachers going?* New York: Teachers College Press.

Noddings, N. (1986). Fidelity in teaching, teacher education, and research for teaching. *Harvard Educational Review, 56*(4), 496–510.

Palmer, P. J. (1998). *The courage to teach: Exploring the inner landscape of a teacher's life.* San Francisco: Jossey-Bass.

Pellicer, L. O., & Anderson, L. W. (1995). *A handbook for teacher leaders.* Thousand Oaks, CA: Corwin Press.

Rogers, F. (2003). *The world according to Mister Rogers.* New York: Hyperion.

Rose, M. (1989). *Lives on the boundary: A moving account of the struggles and achievements of America's educationally underprepared.* New York: Penguin Books.

Sapon-Shevin, M. (1990). Schools as communities of love and caring. *Holistic Education Review, 3*(2), 22–24.

Sergiovanni, T. J. (2001). *The principalship: A reflective practice perspective.* Boston: Allyn & Bacon.

Tileston, D. W. (2004). *What every teacher should know about special learners.* Thousand Oaks, CA: Corwin Press.

Wiggins, G., & McTighe, J. (1998). *Understanding by design.* Alexandria, VA: Association for Supervision and Curriculum Development.

Index

**CORWIN
PRESS**

The Corwin Press logo—a raven striding across an open book—represents the union of courage and learning. Corwin Press is committed to improving education for all learners by publishing books and other professional development resources for those serving the field of PreK–12 education. By providing practical, hands-on materials, Corwin Press continues to carry out the promise of its motto: **"Helping Educators Do Their Work Better."**